Waiting for Epi

Roger Kalter

PublishNation
www.publishnation.co.uk

DEDICATION & ACKNOWLEDGEMENTS

The author would like to express sincere thanks to Carolle for her continuous motivation and kind support during the writing process. Also a big thank you to Norman for his dedicated proofreading and valuable input and appreciation. And to any other friends and colleagues whom I've forgotten to mention. You know who you are!

1

Special thanks to Drew Danburry and MP   Cunningham for permission to use the cover photo.
Danburry Barber Shop
55 North University Avenue #145
Provo, Utah 84601

TABLE OF CONTENTS

WAITING FOR EPI

I'm sitting in the waiting room waiting for the doctor to call me, in order to have a part of my ear cut off! Just a small procedure to remove a small pre-cancerous bump!

It's not really about the ear per se, but rather about the waiting.

My mind floats back to my childhood in the early 50's, when I was sent to the barbershop on my own at the tender age of 6, or there about. My mother sent me, with 50 cents in my pocket, and instructed me very carefully to only have my hair cut by Epi the barber, and by no one else.

New York City in the early 50's was usually safe and peaceful. Young children would often ask adults to "cross" them when crossing major streets. The adult would take the child's hand and accompany them while crossing the street. There was an innocence and trustworthiness back in those days. No risk of lawsuits or hesitation to "do the right thing".

I had come directly to the barbershop after school and I was sitting and waiting my turn to have my monthly haircut. In those days my hair would grow fast and wild. As it said on the bottle of hair lotion that I would occasionally use some mornings, "For unruly hair". It probably also matched my personality, but that's not of interest now.

The various customers would step up into the chair and the barber would snap his scissors and wield his comb with professional ease and 20 to 30 minutes later the entire procedure was completed. The barber looked down at me and motioned that I should hop up to the chair. But he was not Epi. Not wanting to appear disrespectful, I simply indicated that I was ready to wait a bit longer. You see, Epi was not yet in the shop, and I didn't want to create a scene. So I simply waited until he would walk in and take his position behind chair number 3.

An interesting and somewhat disturbing point about this barbershop consisting of 3 Italian immigrants was the water color painting hanging in a prime location facing the customers as they were having their hair cut. This painting, which surely had an impact on young impressionable customers such as myself, remains fixed in my mind and will never be forgotten. It must have been the work of some artist with a twisted mind or sense of humor. This painting was of a young boy, maybe 12 or 13 years old with long curly locks of blond hair and a fair complexion. His head was facing towards the wall, and one could only see the rear of his head with a partial view of his face. What stood out was the image of blood streaming down from his ear where it appeared that scissors had cut him because maybe the boy would not sit still during the haircut procedure. The thought of, "For unruly hair" – and maybe even children always came to mind.

Epi had the typical old-fashioned barber's look. Slicked down thinning hair, combed straight back, his thin gold rimmed spectacles and barber's white smock with a buttoned collar neatly around his neck. A comb and short scissors were placed neatly in his left breast pocket. But Epi wasn't present and I was too naïve to imagine that maybe cutting hair was not the only business these 3 barbers were involved in. After all, there was a curtain hiding the passageway to the back of the shop, and who knows what was going on back there.

I really never liked getting a haircut. Mainly because when the event was over, tiny small hairs were always getting down the back of my shirt and would be so uncomfortable until I got home and could have a shower. One time, I remember having jumped out of the chair half way through the procedure, and ran out of the shop. My father, who had accompanied me that Saturday morning, finally coaxed me back. But yes, I was like the hair lotion bottle said, "For unruly hair" (and children!).

It was now starting to get dark, as it was still winter, and I wanted to get back home but Epi still hadn't come in to the shop. I suppose about two hours had gone by and the last customer had just stepped out of the chair.

"Come on, get in the chair and I'll give you your haircut," the barber said to me with an annoying impatience.

"Ah, well, my mother said that I should only have my hair cut by Epi," I replied respectfully.

The barber looked at me and in a very matter of fact way replied:
"Epi's dead."

ALBERT THE RAT

In all my years of professional work experience, no one showed themselves to be so dishonest and disdainful as Albert, the very incompetent and inefficient manager of our small sales group, embedded within a major globally active telecommunications company. Having held majority shares in a company bought out by this global organization, Albert was politically well placed and so able to do very little and yet remain "in charge". Once, in a tête-à-tête, he explained to me how his 15 years of sales experience enabled him to succeed in his profession of sales manager. I decided not to challenge him on this despite my own 25 years experience in sales, as it would have simply poured oil on the fire, so to speak. However, in the following story you will see that his dastardly behavior and lack of human respect, qualify him quite clearly for the title of Albert the Rat.

As the days and months following my joining the company went by, I realised that very few sales contracts were actually being signed: by my colleagues, or for that matter by Albert. It may very well have been that Albert was only keeping a staff of sales people to justify his own presence as manager. However, some months after settling in, Albert handed over responsibility to me for two major international accounts. This gift was actually a poisoned chalice as the files were full of unanswered requests by the customers dating back 6 months or more; requests for technical specifications and pricing for the different products we offered. None of the requests had been answered and the customers had finally given up trying to engage with our company in order to obtain satisfactory replies. As you may have guessed, these accounts were of course the responsibility our sales manager, Albert.

Well, what was I to do?

It occurred to me that these 2 major accounts had the potential to become an extremely profitable business and, as I was given them without any expectations or objectives, I decided to spend 2 to 3 hours every morning, painstakingly answering these antiquated requests in an attempt to rebuild a relationship with the customers. In just a few months that confidence returned and we were actually receiving orders for telecom connections without ever having to make an offer or discuss pricing details. The accounts needed our service and price was not going to be an issue. Fax orders came in almost on a weekly basis, albeit not for high cost products but nevertheless generating a steady source of revenue for the company. Most importantly, confidence had been restored. As one account was very active in eastern Europe, and there had never been any organized meetings or face-to-face discussions between our counterpart in Moscow, ourselves and the customer, I organized a sales and administration conference in our offices in order to solidify these working relationships. This event attracted attention all the way up the company hierarchy and would now involve the country manager from the headquarters in Zurich as well as the local managing director in our office.

Can you now see where all this was leading? Talk about seeding my own downfall. For despite turning around this hopeless business situation into a very positive result from a company perspective, I had of course made Albert appear totally out of place as a sales manager.

This and other events had upset him so much, that Albert actually cancelled one of my appointments with the other major account, by calling my contact and saying I was not able to come as planned. Albert then told me that the account had phoned to say that they were travelling on that day and would be unavailable. I didn't believe him, so I phoned my contact and he told me that Albert had said that I was unavailable on that day. He also proposed that we should maintain the agreed upon meeting. When I returned to the office, Albert asked me why I had gone to the meeting after he had told me the account was travelling. Well, Albert really had his nose put out of shape so to speak: he was caught in a lie in front of both the sales and all the other employees in our office.

Oh my God, I was setting myself up for a major fall.

The next "shot in my foot" was when Albert invited the entire office to his golf club; a chance to hit some balls, have a fun time followed up with a nice dinner at the end of the day.

This sounded like fun indeed. Albert would have the chance to reveal himself as an accomplished golfer, even if his business acumen was sorely lacking.

As for me, though never a dedicated player I've been playing golf, albeit sporadically, since the age of 12 and so did possess the basic skills.

Driving a golf ball off the tee was never going to be a major challenge. So, against better judgment, I went along with my own set of Wilson clubs and took my place together with my colleagues on the driving range. Most of my colleagues were non-players or real beginners. As it came to my turn to smack the little white ball, Albert was carefully watching. Yes, I hit the ball cleanly and sent it flying straight and true some 200 meters down the imaginary fairway.

" Ah, you've played before," said Albert, slightly embarrassed.

Once again, the lesson to be learned is to never, ever, outperform your boss.

Some weeks later the major account who was now solidly involved with us as a credible supplier of communications infrastructure, contacted me to say that they were renegotiating their contract for Europe-wide telecommunications and that the business would be offered to us or another major supplier. They requested that I come to Paris to make a presentation of how we were organized to take on this project. We certainly had come a long way from the pile of unanswered requests from this customer over 6 months ago: a real turnaround, for sure.

When I informed Albert that we had to prepare for this presentation, his reaction was adamant.

"You're not going to that presentation"

When I asked why, Albert replied that we had to talk together with the country manager from Zurich. I spoke to the country manager and his response was that of course I would be going to Paris to make the presentation: after all it was my client.

All well and good, until the day the three of us were sitting in Albert's office and he quietly announced that I would be fired.

"Why?" asked the country manager.

Albert replied, "Because I say so. I don't need a reason."

As I was escorted out of the office and down the corridor with Albert walking close behind, it readily occurred to me how easy and gratifying it would be to turn around and punch this "Rat" hard and square right in the face. Break that smug and confident, poor excuse of a person and teach him a lesson once and for all. But then, the voice of reason and logic calmed me. It would most likely have been the end of my right to continue living and working in Switzerland.

And so, that's the story of Albert the Rat and me.

PS. Albert never went to Paris and the project was given to our competitor.

THE BIRTHDAY GIFT FROM HELL – NOT REALLY

A birthday is a celebration that supposedly brings joy and cheer to the recipient and denotes the passing of another Earth's orbit around the sun. Oftentimes presents are offered in celebration. As you will discover in this story, the present offered was in fact only a present in a backhanded sort of way!

In my previous book I related how I managed to obtain this interesting position in medical equipment sales working with Mr Obi. Now it became a quarterly event organised by the chairman of the board to have a meeting highlighting equipment sales and turnover. On most of these occasions I was not invited to these events. However, on this one occasion I did participate and discovered that the sales in all regions were in a downward trend apart from my sales region, which was most decidedly moving upward on their graph. This was a surprise to me as every month I was told that I must increase my sales results!

It was clear that my sales area was the only one generating increasing turnover, yet my boss was always giving the impression that my results were not enough, when in reality, it was all the other areas which were in decline.

There were many changes in the management team during my three years with the Kontron/Hoffman la Roche group, and our sales managers were replaced almost every 6 months. The chairman wanted to see increased sales results without ever asking why those in the French speaking area were always increasing while those in the German speaking area were always in decline.

The moment came when the long standing sales manager, Mr Obi, who had hired me almost three years earlier, was asked to leave the company. He had been there as long as anyone in the sales team, but the new sales director Mr Pfister, viewed him as a threat and so it was a political move to get Mr Obi off the team!

This would come back to haunt him in the not so distant future, as Mr Obi would join a competing group and organise a team of his best sales people going forward.

Sales in my area continued to accelerate and I was quite pleased about having taken a rather slow and decidedly forgotten market region to new levels of success month after month. It was, in a way, the foretelling of my downfall.

We were in the town of St. Gallen for a medical equipment exhibition, and who should wander up to our stand, but Mr Obi. He immediately came up to me and in a hushed tone, asked if I was still happy working in his former organisation. I replied that I was more or less OK, but what did he have in mind. He explained that he was putting together a new sales team and that if I would be in agreement, he could make me a very attractive offer. In fact, he had organised for me what would be the most interesting job interview I'd ever had, with his company director and on the day after the closing of the St. Gallen exhibition!

And then, the day before the closing of the St. Gallen exhibition, which actually fell on my birthday, came the request by our new sales manager, Mr Pfister, to meet at the close of the day. Mr Pfister, another colleague and myself walked calmly to the exhibition café and sat in comfortable armchairs and waited for Mr Pfister to begin the discussion, with me all the while thinking it was going to be some birthday recognition. Well, more fool me for thinking that, yet in hindsight, it was indeed a birthday gift of sorts. What followed was a surprise even for my colleague who, as I later learned, came along to be the third party witness. Mr Pfister explained that it was necessary to reduce costs and that my position as sales manager for the Swiss French region was to be terminated and handled from the Zurich office. This would be effective immediately, and I was free to not be in the office but just "around" should my services be required. My colleague was caught totally off guard and responded by telling Mr Pfister, that today was my birthday.

"Oh," said Mr Pfister, "Well, tell me what you would like for your birthday and we'll get it for you."

In reality this was essentially the best gift I could have imagined. Not only was I paid for the months of June, July and August, but I could keep the company car until then as well!

And so, I had my meeting/interview with Mr Obi and Mr von Lanthen for my new job as sales manager for medical equipment in the Swiss French region just as before. But, this time not only did I receive a 13th salary, a free lunch when in the office and a company car, but a commission based on monthly sales.

"Don't even worry about meeting your monthly sales requirement, as sales from our disposable products will easily meet that figure," said Mr von Lanthen.

I really couldn't believe the luck that had befallen me.

After a few months, the company director wanted to sell our aging stock of ultrasound equipment for gynaecology applications. He offered to give a prize of a significant amount to the sales person, anywhere within the company (Europe) who sold the most number of units within a 3-month period.

So, this is what I did. I had a customer base of seven ultrasound users from my previous position, with each unit costing about Sfr 60'000. The unit from my new company was priced at approximately the same level but offered much-improved quality. Our director agreed to buy back all those old units for Sfr 30'000 each and replace them with a leasing agreement totalling Sfr 30'000 per unit. In the end each surgery would receive a discount on our ultrasound unit of Sfr 30'000 and only have to pay a small sum covering the monthly leasing. Within the time frame of three months, I bought back all those units and sold new ones thereby throwing out my previous company's market domination in ultrasound equipment sales in the Swiss French sales area.

I was the "darling" of the company director and I won the contest by selling more than any other sales person in the entire company.
My prize was a portable colour TV set!

I guess you could say that was a great birthday present from Mr Pfister.

THE CHAIR

James Squires, a medical student at the University of Lausanne, was a rather studious example of self-belief. What I mean to say is that he really believed that by talking all about his study habits, he could convince others and himself that he was seriously committed to the pursuit of medical success and achieve his desire to finish medical school by transferring back to his home country, the United States of America.

So it happened that on a particular day, James sat in his usual lunchtime chair in the student cafeteria. Don't get me wrong; this story is not about *that* chair. No, James sat down with his lunchtime tray of food, and started to relate his experience about his visit to the antique furniture shop and the amazing chair he had spotted. He started to tell me that he found the particular chair, which, although a bit expensive for him, was what seemed to be an extremely good and comfortable study chair. He went on and on about how this particular chair would allow him to study in a more effective manner. How this chair would be important to the success of his academic achievements. He said that the shop owner even allowed him to try it out by sitting in it with his textbook and study for a while. Yes, this would be a purchase to seriously consider. After all, it was to be part of his academic pursuit.

James had an appearance of a rather disheveled unkempt young man with little attention regarding how he was perceived.

"Roger, I haven't the time to really trim my moustache, or any of that, I'm here to study and I need to pass my exams to be able to transfer back to med school in the USA," James would tell me between spoonfuls of the "soupe du jour".

James had a handlebar moustache of sorts and a rather unshaven confused face. With his confused look, it was rather dubious that he manifested a positive bedside manner.

"I want to tell you about this chair I've been looking at. The shopkeeper was happy to tell me about the provenance of this antique armchair and I'm pretty sure I want to get it, but it is kind of big and cumbersome, so I have to really think about it. I mean how will I get it to my apartment, etc."

James did mention the possibility of having the chair delivered and he said he would go back the next day and make the request.

It did seem to me that James was spending quite a bit of time analyzing the purchase. Day after day the "marathon" of considerations and hesitations filled James' dissertations and monologue regarding his eventual expenditure for the need to have a chair, which would enable him to have more effective study habits.

The following week James came into the student cafeteria with a resolute smile on his unshaven, confused face.

"I've decided to probably buy that chair. The shopkeeper said to me that he would have it delivered to the apartment if I could decide, and that he would consider a reduced delivery charge."

I could easily imagine that the shopkeeper really was fed up by now with this "studious" young man requiring a comfortable antique armchair in order to pursue his arduous study habits with the objective of passing his exams to transfer back to med school in the USA.

"I need to go back to the shop and see if I can work out a more reasonable price. After all, he really should sell it to me, as I've been so interested. And I really think it will help me to focus on the important purpose of my being here, the study of medicine."

All this seemed to be very reasonable apart from the fact that James still hadn't concluded the purchase of his armchair. In fact, one might believe that this scenario of discussions and shop visits, along with a daily diatribe of "armchair" events, might lead one to believe that James was not at all a med student in search of a medical diploma but rather a very particular shopper. I never really understood his continued ramblings about this stupid chair.

"I can't decide if I really need this chair," he said at lunch during another week of belabored ruminations. "I think I might buy it and then discover it really doesn't suit me. I would only want to get rid of it, sell it, and that would be an inconvenience."

On and on and on, this story seemed as though it would never end. Did James truly want a chair for better studying, or was this just a pretext to avoid the issue at hand, becoming a doctor!

It all came to a stunning conclusion some time the following week. James came in to the cafeteria and sat down at the table across from me.

"So, did you get the chair? Did they deliver it as promised?" I inquired.

"No, I didn't. I am still uncertain as to whether or not the chair really suits my needs."

"I know what you mean. I once was going to invest in a piece of antique furniture and just before buying it …"

James cut me off mid sentence and interjected: "Listen Roger, I can't discuss with you about that, you know I really have no time, I'm a very busy medical student and I really have to just spend my time studying …"

I have no idea if James ever acquired the chair, and I really couldn't care. What I do know is that James was probably so self-centered that, as a medical doctor, he could never have a patient oriented approach! For sure, I would never consult him.

I could just imagine his office, sometime in the future, with a large antique armchair in the corner of the patient waiting room. It would be cordoned off with a sign saying: "This chair is for display only and may not be used."

THE MAGIC GLOVE

This is a story about a magic glove. But not the kind of glove that you might imagine. Not the "Cinderella's-glass-slipper" type of glove. No, this was the Rawlings BT 99 Bob Turley model baseball glove. And it did have some magical qualities.

The winter of 1958-59 in New York City was cold and snowy. On this particular day, after a night of heavy snowfall, the morning's streets were silent and empty. The cold dry powder snow had blanketed the entire island of Manhattan with more than 2 feet of snow, causing schools to be closed and transportation was almost non-existent. It was on these types of day that I would ask the superintendent of our building if I could borrow his shovel. It wasn't a snow shovel, but a rather heavy, iron shovel used for filling the coal-fired furnace that our apartment building used to have. As the building was upgraded to oil heating, Mr Collins didn't use the shovel any longer and would agree to let me use it to shovel snow. It was solidly constructed with a wooden D-shaped handle at the end and a rather heavy iron "pan" with curved edges which was meant to keep the coal in the shovel, but in this case the snow.

I would go around and ring the doorbells of all the tenants in my building and the building across the street, asking if they would need their car shovelled out from under the snow. This day was quite successful and I managed to get 5 clients. This meant 2 to 3 hours of shovelling at 3 dollars a car. Sometimes the snowplough would drive by while clearing the streets, and push all the snow that I had cleared, back in front of the car I was working on. This made my job a little bit more frustrating. I remember finishing the day, exhausted and with soaking feet, because my high rubber boots were not able to keep the deep snow from edging in over the top and sliding down to my thirsty socks. Nevertheless, as I wandered back home in the falling darkness, I was content that on this day I had earned 15 dollars. This was a lot of money back in those days for a 12 year old, whose weekly allowance of pocket money was 1 dollar.

I remember my father being rather upset and saying to my mother, "This is not right; a boy of his age with 15 dollars in his pocket!"

I think he didn't like the idea that this money was able to give me a sense of independence and, as he was rather a "control freak", it made him loose some command over my behaviour.

The winter eased into spring and I could smell the greening in the air as, every day, I walked down the winding hill to the subway station to get the train to school. At school, when the weather warmed up, usually around the end of March or the beginning of April, we would have PhysEd and go to the park to play softball. One of my good friends, Steve Shabad, had a new baseball glove, which he got for the new baseball season. It was an amazing glove. It was the Rawlings BT 99 Bob Turley model. It had a deep pocket, which was also big enough to hold, quite tightly, a softball. This meant that once the ball was caught, it was not about to drop out. I even borrowed it a few times when Steve and I were on opposite sides. Steve usually played at shortstop and I played at 3rd base for which this glove was perfect.

I had to have one. And, as I still had the 15 dollars I made shovelling snow, it would be the perfect birthday gift that I could buy for myself. Steve told me that the glove cost 15 dollars at Macy's, so, a few weeks later on a Friday after school, I took the subway down to 34th street to make my pre-birthday purchase.

I took my glove to summer camp that year and had a great time playing on the camp softball team. We played other camps in the area and had a pretty good record, winning most of our games. I played 3rd base and my Rawlings BT99 glove did a pretty good job of catching line drives down the line. As we had a rather good team, the camp counsellors, the 20-35 year old adults that looked after us, decided to play us in a camper-counsellor softball game. It was obvious that they were a stronger side, but as we practiced almost daily, while they were doing the "supervising" of their various groups, we might stand a chance due to our better team organization.

I was playing left field, in the outfield for this game, as the counsellors usually hit the ball quite far and my throwing ability from deep in left field was going to be needed. Up to the plate came Frank Shrapaway.

Rumour had it that Frank had tried out for a major league baseball team, the Brooklyn Dodgers. But I guess he wasn't good enough. He didn't pass the tryouts and he never mentioned to us what had happened. We had seen many times the power that he displayed when he connected with the ball. It was something awesome. He would hit towering line drives across the playing field deep into the outfield. This truly was major league power.

As Frank came to bat, I immediately moved 20 to 30 yards back, and even then I knew that if he wanted, he could hit the ball over my head for an easy home run. Frank took the second pitch and with a tremendous swing, sent the ball high and long in my direction. I didn't wait around to see how far it was going to go. I simply turned around and ran as fast a I could deeper into the outfield, not even looking to see where the ball was. For some reason, which I will never understand, after about 20 yards, it occurred to me all of a sudden, that I should reach out into the air, without looking up, and hold out my glove. I was like something I had seen in a cartoon, where the animated character reached out in impossible desperation. And so, as if by the hand of God, the ball dropped ever so lightly, almost too lightly, into the pocket of my glove. It startled me that it fell so softly. But the pocket of this model baseball glove was so well formed, there was no way that it would roll out.

I had robbed Frank Shrapaway of a home run. Truly a magic glove indeed.

And the story doesn't end there.

When I returned home from summer camp, I was out hitting baseballs with my friends. I hit them high and far and after 30 minutes or so it was time to let the others have a go. As I went to pick up my baseball glove to take the field, I saw it was gone. I looked around the spot where I had placed it, looked under my jacket, and couldn't imagine that I had lost it. After a minute or so, up strolls this young kid, maybe 9 or 10 years old, and asks me if I had lost my baseball glove. I told him it seemed like it but that I could swear it was there before.

"So, how much would you pay to get it back?" he asked in a business-like manner.

"Well, that was a very good glove and I would pay 2 dollars to the person who could bring it back to me," I said naïvely.

"OK, tell me where you live and if you'll give me 2 dollars, I'll get it back for you."

So I gave him my address and told him to come by at 6 o'clock that evening.

When I got home I told my mother the story and sure enough, at 6 pm the doorbell rang and the kid stood there with my glove. My mother took the glove handed it to me and asked, "Is that your glove?"

"Yes," I replied. "I told him I would pay 2 dollars if he brought it back."

My mother looked at the young thief standing there and summarily slammed the door in his face.

FIRST JOB INTERVIEW AND WHAT I DID TO GET IT

In 1973, way back in the "olden" days before the advent of desktop personal computers and word processing, I created and sent my CV and cover letter to a handful of American companies present in the French speaking area of Switzerland, where I was living at the time. Of course I had no idea that my application would be successful. As they say, you shouldn't hope for something because in the end, you may get it. In this case, was success a curse rather than a blessing? Was I the one being "played"? You be the judge.

In order to "personalize" the application I knew I would have to include the company name in the text. Not really a problem if the letter is a one-off. However, as I was writing to more than a few companies with basically the same text and, as mentioned above, no text processing existed, I simply left a somewhat adequate space to type in the company name in question on the photocopied document. This was all well and good, until I attempted to fill in the space reserved with the name Applied Research

Laboratories. There never was going to be enough place. So, as I typed in the company name in the space I had reserved for this, it was necessary to slightly adjust the text line to actually curve above the already printed line. Not really going to give a good first impression with this, was I? Nevertheless I sent this off with a just as hastily created resume. Those were the days when obtaining a job interview was really quite easy. Even if there were no positions offered, companies would interview candidates, "just to see". The crazy thing was that I had no idea what the company did or anything about them, apart from the fact that they had offices and production facilities only 25 minutes from my home.

You can imagine my surprise when I discovered in my mailbox and invitation to come for an interview at the end of March!

It was a crisp clear day with a blue sky and I knew that I had to wear a suit and tie and shine my shoes in order to at least not appear to be anything that resembled the shoddy cover letter that I had sent. I presented myself at the reception desk and was invited to take a seat and wait for Mr de Beer, who would be seeing me shortly.

About 15 minutes later I was ushered into a typical modern day office and invited to have a chair across from a clean wooden desk, directly facing the window and Mr de Beer.

The building was quite attractive and modern, architecturally equivalent to a strip mall having only one level with a central open grassy area surrounded by offices and a factory for the production of the ARL emission and fluorescence spectrometers.

"So, how did you know or learn about ARL," inquired Mr de Beer with a welcoming smile.
"Or did you just find us in the phone book?"

Naively, I replied that I actually had a book of all Swiss/American companies in the area and sort of sent off my CV to the ones that appeared most interesting.

I don't think he was too impressed by my response, but nevertheless, he continued to explain that ARL manufactured on their premises the industry's highest performing spectrometers. Of course, followed by the inevitable question, did I know what a spectrometer was or what it did? I hesitated and thought back to my Walden School chemistry classes and replied with some sort of a hazy explanation. That seemed to slightly offset the initial impression relating to my "phone book" discovery of their company and Mr de Beer continued to introduce the sales department and its functions. A very interesting statement then followed this.

"Well, Mr Kalter, I don't think we have anything to offer you."

In the interim, I was asked if I would like a coffee, and I replied in the affirmative. I mean, why shouldn't I hang around a while longer sipping a coffee?

And thus continued Mr de Beer's presentation of the marketing and sales department and the various issues and problems he was facing as the department manager. From time to time he would ask me my opinion or thoughts on these issues, to which I replied with a hesitant and slightly perplexed honesty. Why, I asked myself, was he taking the time to ask me, when after all, he must have better things to do with his time. Of course, I didn't, so I just sat and listened.

3 hours and 2 more coffees later Mr de Beer said to me:

"Well, we do have a position of sales engineer for the Eastern European countries. Would you be interested in that?"

At that moment I just replied, "Yes."

After a short exchange of details, Mr de Beer picked up the phone and called down the corridor to the personnel department and said to draw up a contract for me and that I was to start at the beginning of the following month, April 1st.

Seems that this was rather simple and straightforward. Photocopy a standard letter, regardless of spacing and format and obtain an interview. What could have possibly created the curiosity and interest of Mr de Beer to actually offer me a challenging and interesting position with a major international organization, after such a one-sided 3-hour "discussion"?

Nevertheless this sales engineer position was quite a challenge. As a young, naive and inexperienced 25 year old, I was sent off on sales trips to all the major Eastern European communist countries visiting the production laboratories, when permitted. Of course carrying boxes of sales brochures, etc. meant that travel could only reasonably be done by car. This meant that I had to be prepared to drive many hours crossing boarders and checkpoints making my way to the outlying regions away from the city centers. Perhaps this was the reason they offered me the position. Not many people would accept to be away from home for 2 or more weeks in these remote regions. I must admit, there was a lot to learn from the standpoint of commercial dealings in these countries. Not at all like what goes on in western capitalist economies. In my previous book, "Valuta in the Cover" many of these adventures are recounted to the amazement of many readers.

So in conclusion, I must admit that up until this writing, I always honestly believed that I obtained this position because of a successful interview based on my ability to listen more and talk less.

But the reality may actually have been that I was "ripe for the picking", that's to say full of youthful enthusiasm and naive enough to allow myself to be sent off on lonesome and occasionally risky sales trips in many "uncharted" territories.

You be the judge, what do you believe?

A HOLE-IN-ONE DONUT

I've always liked donuts. I remember going to the corner drugstore at school lunch break and having a chocolate covered donut and a Coke with my school friend Steve back in New York City.

In those days nobody worried about calories. We were quite active as youngsters growing up in the city. Little did I realize that those lunch-break trips to the corner drugstore would set the tone for a marketing adventure some 40 years later.

Living and working in Switzerland is quite enjoyable and rewarding, with a standard of living that surpasses many modern western countries. In fact, the cost of living would leave many of my American compatriots wide eyed and open mouthed when viewing the prices in the local supermarkets. Nevertheless, with the high cost of living, many traditional products found in the shops in my homeland are often non-existent here in the land of cheese and chocolate. For many years peanut butter was unknown. So was ketchup, and even today in 2017, American yellow mustard is a rarity. It was in 1980, or there about, that Macdonald's began to sell donuts in their UK burger chain. They were quite good and I always would get some when in the UK. Saying that I often thought that what Switzerland needed was a good donut shop.

The idea occurred to me to see if I could find a decent recipe for this pastry delight. Would it be as popular in Switzerland as elsewhere? And so the search was on and the idea of creating Switzerland's first donut shop was in the planning stage.

Firstly, I was on the lookout for a good donut recipe. Next, I would need a donut fryer. I was able to find a basic recipe and tweak it a bit to correspond to my needs. In the process I learned quite a bit about the baking business. I had no idea, for example, that I could replace fresh eggs with powdered yolks to achieve the same result, as the yolk was only needed as a binding agent. Also, the biggest secrets of creating the perfect donut are the oil temperature and the frying time. This had to be very precise otherwise catastrophe was inevitable.

The donut machine arrived from the USA where I ordered it from and, funnily enough, it was called Hole in One! This would be the name used for my donut shop. I handled the entire set-up process myself. I even took the photos of donuts on a white saucer with a cup of hot black espresso on a clean white tablecloth. Five sorts of donut topping would be created; chocolate, vanilla, vanilla with chocolate sprinkles, plain, and the luxurious cinnamon with powdered sugar. That was the top seller, a true masterpiece when warm and fresh.

The next step was to secure contracts to deliver freshly made donuts daily to the major international companies located in the area. First was Phillip Morris, the world's second largest food company. So, off I went, a box of donuts in hand to meet with the cafeteria manager. We sat down, had a sample of these gastronomic delicacies and, believe it or not, they placed an order for daily deliveries! Wow, unbelievable. Next was Nestlé. Same scenario, and they also placed an order for daily deliveries. And the shop wasn't even open yet! I also managed to have a postal delivery to a well-known Japanese school in Leysin with the help of the Swiss postal service. I guess donuts are big stuff in Japan, who would have thought?

And so, the day arrived for the shop's grand opening. And, after a few hours, we sold out the entire morning's production – a sign of things to come.

At one point, an American who lived in the area discovered our existence. He was so pleased to see American donuts being made and sold just down the street from where he lived. He began asking many questions about this adventure, recalling how he had always loved donuts and how pleased he was to discover this culinary delight. He continued to ramble on for about 20 minutes. Finally, I asked him if he would like to take some home to try later.

"Are these cake donuts or yeast donuts?" he inquired.

"These are cake donuts," I replied.

" Oh, I don't like cake donuts," and out he walked!

SMELLS LIKE ASIAN CUISINE – FIRE IN THE HOUSE

It was already a few weeks into the fall semester and I had returned to my rented room from an early morning class. It was a room in a two-story house just off campus and I had one of the three rooms on the second floor above a normal flat downstairs. The air was crisp and there was snap in the cold dry temperature, which indicated that despite the month of October, cold winter weather was soon to be upon us.

I returned from an early morning class and was free until the afternoon, so I decided to crack open a textbook and do some studying for a change. I really had no idea what was about to happen that morning which could have seriously impacted not only my school life but the other residents of this rented house as well.

Living off-campus was a good way to keep your independence by not having to rely on and pre-pay for a semester of dormitory cafeteria meals and dormitory living conditions, for example, no female visitors, no cooking hot plates, etc. So, many students opted for the off-campus solution. In my particular situation I had rented a room along the road just opposite some of the campus dormitories, so there was access, if need be, to dormitory facilities. So, all in all, it was quite a convenient solution.

As I continued reading one of my boring textbooks (probably the Legal and Constitutional History of England), I noticed a rather strange smell coming from the hallway just outside my room. I continued reading not really giving any more thought to this aroma or its possible origin.

Nevertheless, the scent continued to increase, as did my curiosity as to what the hell my neighbor was cooking for lunch. It was a growing pungent and overpowering odor that eventually motivated me to walk over to his room and knock on his door. But there was no answer! I knocked again and now decided to turn the doorknob to make sure everything was all right. Well, it wasn't. As I opened the door I was immediately engulfed in thick black smoke coming from a burning mattress. I began to fill a rubbish bin with water from the adjacent bathroom in order to douse the flames, but to no avail. The smoke was too thick and it was impossible to enter the room.

Off I ran across the street to the MSU dorm, requesting the front desk to immediately call the fire department, as I had no phone in my room. The bozo at the desk, completely out of his depth, said he couldn't call the campus fire department for an off-campus fire, and that the desk phone could only make on-campus phone calls. A moment of reflection, and I could imagine this old wood structure going up like matchsticks if something wasn't done immediately. I didn't hesitate to instruct this airhead to call the campus fire department, which in turn would alert the East Lansing fire department to rush over to 135 Bogue Street and put out the flames!

And so he did, thank goodness. They arrived in five minutes, entered the room, threw the mattress out the window down to the backyard as black smoke bellowed from the broken window and all was finished – for now!

That evening, as the smoke and most of the smell had dissipated from the house, I was quietly sitting in my room thinking about what might have been. As no one was in the house but me, the entire wooden structure could have gone up in flames. All my clothes, books and other belongings would have been totally lost. Insurance claims and all the other administrative details, along with attending classes would become a major issue. So, it was a good thing I had come home from class that morning. Lauren, whose room was saved from the fire, had a lot to be thankful for. He apparently left his cooking burner on and the cable got too hot and set the mattress on fire. That was all that was damaged, but it easily could have been a lot worse. As it happened, the fire department and police were at the scene! Why? I really didn't know, but the answer would reveal itself shortly. Around six o'clock that evening there was a knock on Lauren's door.

"This is officer Brown of the East Lansing police department, I have a warrant for your arrest for the illegal possession of marijuana!"

And so, Lauren spent the night in prison until released on bail the next day. In spite of this, he did thank me for saving from the flames the room and all the other items that could have been lost.

VALUTA IN THE HUNGARIAN COUNTRYSIDE

I wish I could say that Valuta was the name of this attractive, shapely country maiden that I met while driving across Hungary on my way to Romania. But alas, it was something a bit more careless.

My travels throughout Eastern Europe were in the context of my job, which was a sales engineer for an American manufacturer of laboratory spectrometers used in the production of metal alloys for various industries. So my travels to these countries, in the early '70's was at the height of the cold war and I was an American, living in Switzerland, travelling behind the Iron Curtain. Was I a spy, working clandestinely for the USA? Hardly, but you could easily think that to be the case.

In fact, when I was in Prague, some months before, staying at the Hotel Adler just off Wenceslas Square, I was sleeping in my room after dinner, and suddenly awoke to see a light coming from the hall outside my room. Was there someone coming in or going out of my room. I was frozen in fear. The shadow of the door closed, and I realised that they were going out. I remained perfectly still and waited a few seconds, to be sure no one was keeping me company, and then went to the door and opened it. It was still locked! I looked down the hallway and it was empty. I realised later that I had been dreaming in German. I hardly spoke any German, but in this dream the language flowed, and I wasn't stumbling for words at all. The dream was about me being asked all these technical questions about how our spectrometers worked. Amazingly, I was quite fluent and precise with my answers, and felt somewhat proud of my technical knowledge. Of course, I only realised later, that I must have been drugged during my dinner at the hotel restaurant, and maybe injected with some kind of "truth serum" while I lay in my drugged sleep. The Czech police were asking me all these questions to determine if I was truly a sales person and not something else. I guess I woke up too soon after they had finished (maybe they gave me another drug to wake me up after the truth serum) and that is when I saw the hall light shining into my hotel room. Who knows if that is what really happened? All I can say is that I never dreamt in German before or after that incident.

This time I was on my way to Romania. We always went by car because not only did we take with us boxes full of brochures about the equipment, but most of the visits were to the production facilities in factories far away from the city centres. So, as GPS wasn't invented yet, I had to learn how to read local maps, and speak a bit of the local language to ask directions. Which brings to mind a funny story. In Prague I was often confused by the road signs. Once, when following the directions to Vienna the next road sign, some 10 kms later, showed Vienna to be in the opposite direction! When I asked a local about that, he told me with a laugh, that when the Russians invaded Czechoslovakia in the spring of 1968, the local Czechs would turn all the road signs the wrong way so the invading tanks would not have an easy time getting around. As all the locals knew the roads anyway, they never bothered turning them back again!

But, now I was on my way to Romania, via Vienna, Austria and in order to not have to get an entry visa for Hungary, and change money for the minimum required number of days, I got a transit visa, which allowed me 24 hours and no requirement to change dollars for Hungarian forints. I needed to plan my itinerary very carefully. I needed to drive across the entire country with only one tank of gas as I hadn't planned to have any local currency to buy fuel along the way – credit cards at gas stations were still a long way off in the future.

I arrived in Budapest, coming from Vienna, sometime around 6 pm. I stopped for dinner and filled my gas tank at the only filling station in town where you could pay with US dollars. As darkness began to fall, I headed in the direction of the main road (there were 2, a high road and a more southerly low road) which was the charted route I had marked out to make it across Hungary to the Romanian border town of Arad. Some 3 or 4 hours later I noticed that the towns that I was passing through were not the ones that I had marked on my map. In fact I realised that I had mistakenly taken the more southerly low road and this was a problem. It would not take me to the border crossing I had planned, and even worse, I would not have enough gas. So I had to 1, change some money to buy gas and 2, get back on the main road. Somewhere along this road I stopped in a small café and asked if they could change some dollars for forints. They told me that they couldn't but that a few kms further on, there was a café at a crossroads. They could change my money and taking the road north would lead me to the main road I wanted to be on. There would also be a gas station.

I got back in my car and headed down the road. After half an hour or so, I came upon the crossroads and the all important café. As I drove up I was a bit surprised to see a couple of simple horse-drawn carriages tied up to a hitching post, just like in the cowboy films on television. It was really weird. "Is this the place?" I wondered. It didn't look at all like a place that was going to do banking! Out in the middle of nowhere. But I really had no choice so in I walked. Firstly, I saw a middle aged man filling glass mugs with beer from a garden hose pipe: non-stop. Next I saw short women with tightly knotted black hair and ruddy complexions sitting at tables in the rather large beer hall. There were three musicians playing typical gypsy czardas on their violins. This was a typical rustic country scene literally in the middle of nowhere, lost somewhere on a back crossroads in the Hungarian farmland. I was most distinctly out of place!

But here I was, and I had to do my best. So, I asked the man with the hose pipe if this was correct that I could in fact, change currency and buy some Hungarian forints. He said yes, I could, and how much did I want to exchange. I said I needed to change 10 dollars in order to buy gas at the next gas station, and that I had a transit visa. He reassured me that this was OK and I should give him my passport and the 10 dollars I wanted to change. I was relieved, that I had come to the right place. Or, had I?

He took my passport and the 10 dollars and disappeared behind a wall, and left me standing there. Looking around and realising that 10 minutes or so had passed, it occurred to me that maybe, this had not been such a good idea. "Oh, my God," I told myself, "Not only did I give away my US passport to a total stranger in the middle of the Hungarian countryside, but 10 dollars as well. What a naïve idiot I was." Already I started calculating that I would have enough gas to make it back to Budapest, and I would go to the US embassy the next day and explain what I had done and what had happened. All kinds of scenarios were passing through my head. Finally, I decided to see what was behind the wall, and what was happening. I stepped behind the wall, and there at the end of the passageway, was a big German Sheperd guard dog sitting up and staring at me. A few steps before it, was a dim light shining from a doorway. I gathered up my courage, fearing that the dog would certainly bark and growl. After all, it was a guard dog. As I approached, trying to be fearless and sure of my steps I arrived at the doorway. My attitude must have been sensed by the dog as it didn't bark or growl. In the room beyond was the man who had taken my money and passport, tapping on an electronic calculator, figuring out how many forints he needed to give me. When he finished, he handed me my passport, my Hungarian money and a legal receipt for the exchange. And so this was my experience with valuta in the Hungarian countryside.

About the author

Roger Kalter was born in 1946 in New York City where after spending 3 years at PS 98 public school until the age of 9, when his family entered him at The Walden School. A private progressive education school focussing on the development of the arts and communication skills. He stayed at Walden until his family moved to Michigan when he was 16.

"Walden has always been a major influence in my education and has resulted in creating many meaningful human relationships with teachers and classmates. I owe a lot to the school's teaching philosophy and even to this day, I find myself referring to my experiences there."

After graduating high school in Midland, Michigan, he moved with his family to Zurich, Switzerland and returned to the US to receive his BA degree in social science and law at Michigan State University, in 1968.

He returned to Lausanne, Switzerland at that time, attending courses in social sciences and business at the Université de Lausanne in order to perfect French and ultimately permanently reside there.

Roger was married and has two adult sons and he now makes his home in Aigle, Switzerland just a short way form the Lake of Geneva. As of 2017 Roger is now a full-fledged Swiss citizen

This collection of short stories relate events and circumstances of true life throughout the growing up and formative years, as well as his adult experiences in private and professional surroundings.

This is the second published collection of short stories. (2013 "Valuta in the Cover "

www.ingramcontent.com/pod-product-compliance
Lightning Source LLC
Chambersburg PA
CBHW061221180526
45170CB00003B/1093